Post-War Southern in East Sussex and Kent

Featuring the Photographs of Geoffrey Bloxam

Text by Ian Drummond

Holne Publishing

© Holne Publishing, Ian Drummond & Peter Bloxam 2014
British Library Cataloguing in Publication Data
A record for this book is available from the British Library
ISBN 978-0-9563317-9-3
Published by: Holne Publishing, PO Box 343, LEEDS, LS19 9FW
Typeset by: Holne Publishing Services, PO Box 343, LEEDS, LS19 9FW
Printed by: Charlesworth Press, Flanshaw Way, Flanshaw Lane, Wakefield, WF2 9LP

First Published 2014

Unless otherwise indicated all photographs in this volume are by G.F. Bloxam, copyright P.F. Bloxam, unauthorised reproduction prohibited.

Photographs in this volume have been digitally adjusted to enhance clarity, and also remove blemishes, dust etc. However, no intentional alterations have been made to affect their historical significance.

Unless otherwise indicated for all maps north is at their top edge.

Holne Publishing
PO Box 343
LEEDS
LS19 9FW
enquiries@holnepublishing.co.uk
www.holnepublishing.co.uk

Cover Photos:
Front: On 28 June 1947 Stroudley *Terrier* No.2635, formerly named *Morden*, stands at Brighton works. It had just been repainted in the old London, Brighton and South Coast Railway Improved Engine Green livery when it became the works shunter.

Back: A rural scene on the Hythe branch as ex-South Eastern and Chatham Railway (SECR) class H No.31520 heads the 2.50 pm from Hythe to Sandling Junction which has just passed through the Hayne Wood tunnel on 13 May 1950.

Contents

Above: A picture that seems to encapsulate the light railway scene at Tenterden Town station on the Kent and East Sussex Railway. *Terrier* No.32659 has arrived with the 8.15 am from Robertsbridge consisting of a single coach and a brake van on 17 May 1952.

Acknowledgements

As ever I am grateful to all those who have helped with this album including Lawrie Bowles, Alan Doe, my wife Di, and the staff at the National Railway Museum Search Engine.

Foreword

This book is a tribute in memory of my late brother, Geoffrey Fraser Bloxam, who died in February 1976 at the early age of 48, after a lengthy and debilitating illness.

He was a lifelong railway enthusiast. I have a photo of him when he was about 13, wearing short trousers, on a platform at Clapham Junction surrounded by much older teenagers, including Arthur Nicholls. Arthur is now over 90, and one of a small number who knew Geoffrey and are still with us.

Geoffrey was a member of the RCTS (Railway Correspondence and Travel Society) and the Stephenson Locomotive Society for most of his adult life and a frequent participant in the shed visits and railtours they arranged.

His numerous friends and fellow railway devotees included such well-known personalities as Sid Nash, Derek Winkworth, John L. Smith (Lens of Sutton), Ken Carr, Rev. J.E.T. Phillips, along with enginemen Bert Hooker of Nine Elms Shed and driver Cambray of Salisbury, a regular

(Photographer Unknown)

Atlantic Coast Express performer. All of these have now departed this life.

Very few of the photos reproduced in this book have been published before, and are of such good quality that they deserve to be put together for the first time.

I am grateful to Ian Drummond for the time and energy he has devoted to this volume, and hope it will revive happy memories for all who remember these scenes from over 60 years ago. Younger readers will, I hope, find them of interest also.

Peter F. Bloxam

Introduction

The history of this book goes back to the first volume of *Southern Rails on the Isle of Wight*, when I was seeking the copyright holder of some photos produced by Pamlin Prints. On the reverse of the originals was the name G.F. Bloxam, who was evidently the photographer. Some research later and I was put in touch with Peter Bloxam, Geoffrey's brother.

He, as it transpired, not only held his brother's collection of photographs, but also had a large number of pictures which he had taken. Some of these have been seen in previous volumes in the *Southern Rails* series.

However, Peter was keen that a volume of his brother's photographs should be published, and so I went to see the extent of the collection. What immediately struck me was not only the number of photographs Geoffrey had taken, but also that a significant number of them covered the period of the immediate post-war years. This was a time of significant upheaval on the railways with the disappearance of the 'Big Four' and the advent of British Railways, with all the changes that brought.

However, on the Southern there were still many examples of pre-grouping locomotives in service, many of which would begin to disappear during the 1950s. Therefore, the concept of this album was born.

In it we have concentrated on those photographs of Geoffrey's taken in the years 1946 to 1955, although we have made an exception for the section on the Westerham branch.

In addition, we have limited the geographical area in this volume to east Sussex and Kent, where much of

Geoffrey's early photography took place.

His early photographs took place on shed visits to locations such as Brighton, Eastbourne and Tunbridge Wells. Subsequently he was to photograph trains on the lines of the former London, Brighton and South Coast Railway (LBSCR) in east Sussex. This included an visit to the Kemp Town branch in Brighton.

Later photographs include some of the branches of the former South Eastern Railway (SER) (later the South Eastern and Chatham (SECR)). These include the New Romney and Westerham branches.

He also visited one of the oldest railways in the country between Canterbury and Whitstable to witness the scene at Whitstable Harbour. In addition there were several visits to the Kent and East Sussex Railway.

This, as has been said, was a period of rapid change on the railways, seen in part in the livery variations on the locomotives and carriages. However, it was also a time when Britain's railway map would be changed forever with the closure of many branches and secondary lines. While it is often supposed that this did not really occur until the 'Beeching' cuts of the 1960s, the reality was that the process was well under way in the 1950s.

Therefore, seeking to capture the last days of some of these lines, Geoffrey travelled to places such as the Isle of Sheppey and the Hythe branch to see some of the final trains run. This means that many of these photographs are historical documents, capturing scenes that will not be witnessed again.

Ian Drummond

Brighton lines in East Sussex and Kent

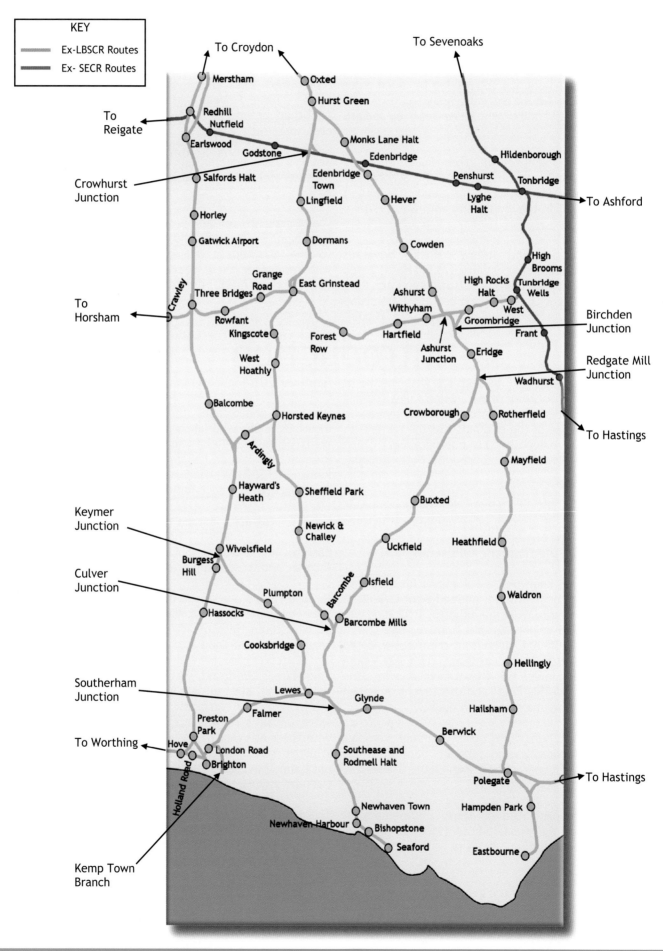

KEY
Ex-LBSCR Routes
Ex- SECR Routes

To Croydon

To Sevenoaks

Merstham

Oxted

Hurst Green

To Reigate

Redhill
Nutfield

Earlswood
Godstone

Monks Lane Halt
Edenbridge

Hildenborough

Crowhurst Junction

Salfords Halt

Edenbridge Town

Penshurst
Tonbridge

To Ashford

Horley

Lingfield

Hever

Lyghe Halt

Gatwick Airport

Dormans

Cowden

High Brooms

Grange Road

East Grinstead

Ashurst

High Rocks Halt
Tunbridge Wells

To Horsham

Three Bridges

Crawley

Rowfant

Withyham
Hartfield

West Groombridge

Birchden Junction

Frant

Kingscote

Forest Row

Ashurst Junction

Eridge

Redgate Mill Junction

West Hoathly

Wadhurst

Balcombe

Horsted Keynes

Crowborough

Rotherfield

To Hastings

Ardingly

Mayfield

Hayward's Heath

Sheffield Park

Buxted

Keymer Junction

Newick & Chailey

Uckfield

Heathfield

Wivelsfield

Burgess Hill

Culver Junction

Plumpton

Barcombe

Isfield

Waldron

Hassocks

Barcombe Mills

Cooksbridge

Hellingly

Southerham Junction

Lewes

Glynde

Hailsham

Falmer

Preston Park

Berwick

To Worthing

Hove

London Road

Southease and Rodmell Halt

Holland Road

Brighton

Polegate

To Hastings

Newhaven Town

Hampden Park

Newhaven Harbour

Bishopstone

Seaford

Eastbourne

Kemp Town Branch

Oxted to Tunbridge Wells West

Frequently during the time period of this book Geoffrey spent days photographing the former LBSCR secondary routes in east Sussex and west Kent, taking full advantage of his lineside pass to obtain images of pre-grouping steam in action. The photographs he took on those occasions form the first sections of this book, which we've assembled into a series of photographic journeys, moving roughly from north to south across the area.

These journeys start on the line Geoffrey photographed the most, the route between Oxted, which is of course actually in Surrey, and Tunbridge Wells West. The history of this route began with the construction of the Croydon, Oxted and East Grinstead Railway.

This was a joint venture between the LBSCR and the SER. It was jointly owned between Croydon and Crowhurst Junction, where the line connected with the SER's Redhill to Tonbridge line, the LBSCR owning the the remainder of the route to East Grinstead. It was opened on 10 March 1884.

To connect with this line at Oxted, the Oxted and Groombridge Railway was promoted. This would form a junction with the route between Tunbridge Wells West and East Grinstead opened in 1866, and also the line from Tunbridge Wells to Uckfield and Lewes, at Groombridge. Originally promoted as a separate company it was absorbed by the LBSCR before the line opened in stages in 1888.

This gave the LBSCR a direct route between London and Tunbridge Wells. However, it was not to be until 1914 that there would be a link through to the Lewes and Eastbourne lines, allowing direct running through from Oxted without the need to reverse at Groombridge. Intermediate stations on the route were provided at Edenbridge Town, Hever, Cowden and Ashurst. Later when railmotors were briefly introduced halts were opened at Hurst Green and Monks Lane in 1907, the latter only lasting until 1939, while the former was resited in 1961.

Most of the line is still open. The section between Oxted and Ashurst Junction is part of the line from London to Uckfield. Meanwhile the section of the route from Groombridge to Tunbridge Wells is now part of the preserved Spa Valley Railway. Only the section from Ashurst Junction to Groombridge has been closed on 5 January 1969.

Above: At*lantic* tank class I3 No.2089 at Oxted with the 3.35 pm to Brighton on 15 May 1948.

Above: *Atlantic* class H2 No.32422 *North Foreland* built 1911 at Oxted on 15 May 1948. This loco had been the first to be painted in lined malachite green by Brighton works in March 1946, with the British Railways lettering and numbering applied over the top following nationalisation. As we shall see Geoffrey clearly had a soft spot for these locos.

Above: An interloper as ex-LMS 2-6-4 tank No.42198 stands at Oxted with the 3.52 pm from Victoria to Brighton on 12 June 1948. This locomotive was then taking part in exchange trials on the Southern Region along with No.42199.

Above: On 28 July 1951 class H2 No.32425 *Trevose Head* shunts the 8.22 am Lewes to London Bridge into a siding due to a hot box. Note the coal merchants' signs on the right, the one for Hall & Co. also proclaiming they sell gravel and lime.

Above: After departing from Oxted with the 3.35 pm to Brighton on 30 June 1951 class I1x 4-4-2T No.2002 crosses Limpsfield viaduct just south of the station. This locomotive was built in 1907 as part of a second batch of ten of the Marsh designed I1 class. It was rebuilt with a larger boiler by the Southern in May 1931 when it was designated as an I1x. Sadly it was to last only a few more weeks in service, being the last of the class to be withdrawn.

Above: Class I3 *Atlantic* tank No.32091 waits for signals just outside Oxted with the 2.34 pm to Tunbridge Wells West, formed with push and pull set No.652, on 5 May 1951. By this time No.32091 has received the 'unicycling lion' early BR totem. It was to be the last of the class in service but was withdrawn in May 1952.

Above: South of Oxted was the 550 yard Limpsfield tunnel where on 30 June 1951 Maunsell designed class U1 No.31903 with the 1.42 pm London Bridge to Tonbridge is about to enter the north portal. No.31903 was built by the Southern in 1931 and lasted in service until 1962.

Above: Class H 0-4-4T No.31279 built in 1909 emerges from the northern portal of Limpsfield tunnel with the 1.20 pm motor train from Tunbridge Wells West to Oxted on 30 June 1951.

Above: South of Limpsfield tunnel was Hurst Green Halt, opened on 1 June 1907, after which came Hurst Green Junction where the lines to East Grinstead and Tunbridge Wells West diverged. Q class No.30533 is seen with the 6.30 pm from Tunbridge Wells to Victoria having passed the distant signal approaching the junction on 10 June 1950.

Above: Beyond Hurst Green *Atlantic* tank No.32022 is photographed with the 4.11 pm Lewes to Victoria having emerged from the north portal of Edenbridge tunnel on 22 April 1950. Edenbridge tunnel was in fact two tunnels with the two parts separated only by an overbridge which carried the Redhill to Tonbridge line. The train is now approaching Monks Lane overbridge, the site of Monks Lane Halt which was open between 1907 and 1939.

Above: Class J1 No.32325, also on the 4.11 pm from Lewes to Victoria, approaches Edenbridge Town on 29 May 1950 having just crossed over the river Eden. This is a locomotive we will be seeing more of.

Above: Now looking north at the same spot as previously, class U1 No.31899 passes with the 4.44 pm from East Croydon to Tonbridge complete with what looks like two milk tankers chained to a pair of flat wagons.

Above: Geoffrey clearly liked this location as, now looking south again, Q classes Nos.30527 and 30533 are captured hauling the 6.30 pm from Tunbridge Wells West to London Victoria.

Above: Class J1 No.32325 (definitely one of Geoffrey's favourite engines) north of Ashurst station with the 4.11 pm from Lewes to Victoria on 3 June 1950.

Above: Looking north from Ashurst station footbridge as class U1 No.31898 enters with the 4.44 pm from East Croydon to Tonbridge on 7 August 1950. The train is crossing a short viaduct which carried the line over a mill race, while further in the distance is another short viaduct over the River Medway.

Above: At the southern end of Ashurst station on 5 August 1950 class U1 No.31894 passes through with the 4.50 pm working from London Victoria to Brighton. Meanwhile in the bay road ex-SECR class D No.1730 waits to depart with the 6.09 pm train from Ashurst to Tonbridge. The class D's were designed by Wainwright for express passenger working, No.1730 was originally built by Sharp, Stewart & Co. in 1901 and would last in service until March 1951.

Above: After the class U1 cleared the section No.1730 sets out for Tonbridge with a train consisting of set No.652 (seen previously on page 10). At this time this set consisted of an ex-London and South Western Railway (LSWR) 50ft composite which had been reframed at Lancing in 1935 and made into a nine-compartment third carrying No.1, and ex-LSWR brake third No. 6428. During the Dunkirk evacuation in September 1939, No.1730 was spotted on the line between Redhill and Reading hauling a train of 14 LMS corridor coaches, a somewhat heavier load than set No.652.

Above: South of Ashurst station *Atlantic* class I3 tank No.32028 heads the 10.54 am from Oxted to Tunbridge Wells West on 4 March 1950. Further down the route came Ashurst Junction where the line from East Grinstead joined from the west, and the lines for Tunbridge Wells and Eastbourne diverged.

Above: Ex-SECR class H No.31550 is seen near Ashurst Junction with the 4.45 pm from Tunbridge Wells West to Ashurst on 21 April 1951.

Above: Groombridge Junction was where the lines from Oxted and East Grinstead joined those from Lewes and Eastbourne for the run into Tunbridge Wells. Here ex-SECR class D No.31586 takes the road for Lewes and Brighton with the 12.36 pm departure from Tunbridge Wells West on 1 April 1950.

Above: Just beyond the junction lay Groombridge station and here on the same day class D No.31734 with the 12.05 pm from Brighton to Tonbridge meets class I3 No.32079 with the 1.08 pm from Tunbridge Wells West to London Bridge.

Above: Class D1/M 0-4-2T No.2253, built in 1882 and originally named *Pelham*, is seen near High Rocks halt with the 12.58 pm from Oxted to Tunbridge Wells West on 1 August 1949. This locomotive was destined to only remain in service a few more weeks being withdrawn the following month.

Above: On 2 July 1950 class E4 No.32480 approaches Tunbridge Wells West with the 10.22 am from Eastbourne. The train seems to be an interesting mix of stock. The E4s were 0-6-2 mixed traffic tank locomotives, designed by Robert Billinton, with 6ft driving wheels. No.32480 was originally built in 1898 and named *Fletching*.

Above: An ex-LSWR interloper, as class T9 No.312 arrives at Tunbridge Wells West with a train from Victoria on 6 June 1949. The station building and clock tower still survive although sadly it is no longer a station.

Above: On 9 August 1947 class D3 0-4-4T No.2395, originally named *Gatwick* when it was built in 1896, awaits its next duty at Tunbridge Wells West.

Above: On 17 May 1948 class I3 *Atlantic* tank No.2022 stands at Tunbridge Wells West with a train for Lewes. No.2022 had been the first of the class to be superheated having been fitted with a modified class B4 boiler when it was built in 1908.

Above: Class J1 No.2325 is seen on 17 May 1948 in its lined Southern malachite green livery with the 2.02 pm train to Lewes. This was a few months before its derailment at Lewes recorded on page 58.

Tunbridge Wells West to East Grinstead

Having reached Tunbridge Wells West the next journey is along the line from there to East Grinstead. Geoffrey made a number of trips along the route, and again captured the variety of trains which could be seen on what was very much a secondary line.

Its history went back further than the route between Oxted and Groombridge, because the line from East Grinstead was the first LBSCR one to reach Tunbridge Wells. Originally promoted by the East Grinstead, Groombridge and Tunbridge Wells Railway Co., it was authorised by Act of Parliament on 7 August 1862. This would run from from East Grinstead where it made an end-on connection with the line to Three Bridges, to Groombridge via Forest Row, Hartfield and Withyham where stations were to be built.

At Groombridge the intention was to join the line of the already authorised Brighton, Uckfield and Tunbridge Wells Railway for the run through to a new station on the western side of Tunbridge Wells. In the event both the East Grinstead and Uckfield companies were absorbed by the LBSCR in 1864. This, combined with delays in the construction of the line from Uckfield to Groombridge, also meant that it was effectively the East Grinstead line that was the first to reach Tunbridge Wells, opening throughout on 1 October 1866.

For all of its life the line between East Grinstead and Groombridge was single track, with a crossing loop added at Forest Row in 1897. The section from Groombridge to Tunbridge Wells was though double tracked. West of Forest Row there was also a long climb at 1 in 80 known as Brambletye bank, and some 880 yard radius curves before the line reached East Grinstead.

A link was later opened between the LBSCR and SER lines in Tunbridge Wells. This formed a end-on junction at the LBSCR station, and allowed for through running to take place between the two systems.

When railmotors were introduced on the Oxted to Tunbridge Wells West services, a new halt was opened at High Rocks between Groombridge and Tunbridge Wells West on 1 June 1907. This was closed on 5 May 1952. Grouping had little effect on the line save for the renaming of the station at Tunbridge Wells to Tunbridge Wells West on 22 August 1923.

Eventually the line between East Grinstead and Groombridge was closed on 1 January 1967. However, as already noted, the line on to Tunbridge Wells survived under BR until 1985, and is now part of the Spa Valley Railway.

Above: Maunsell Q class No.30540 near Ashurst Junction with the 10.45 am from London Bridge to Tunbridge Wells West via Oxted and East Grinstead on 4 March 1950, arrival time at Tunbridge Wells West would be 12.38 pm. Smokebox door numberplates were an addition to ex-Southern locomotives after nationalisation.

Above: On 21 April 1951 Q class No.30541 is seen near the previous spot but going in the other direction with the 4.55 pm from Tunbridge Wells West to Three Bridges.

Above: Geoffrey photographed an unusual form of double-heading on 21 April 1951 as No.32082, the train loco on the 10.45 am from London Bridge to Tunbridge Wells West, was assisted from East Grinstead by fellow class I3 member No.32028, even though the latter had to run bunker first.

Above: Again near Ashurst Junction, the bracket home signal for which can just be made out in the background, on 21 April 1951 class E4 No.32582 heads west with the 3.28 pm goods from Tunbridge Wells West to Three Bridges.

Above: A complete ex-SECR train as class H No.31016 heads a three-coach 'birdcage' set on the 2.19 pm from Tunbridge Wells West to Three Bridges between Ashurst Junction and Withyham on 3 June 1950.

Above: A short goods train is hardly taxing class E4 No.32520 on the 3.28 pm freight from Tunbridge Wells West to Three Bridges near Ham Farm, Withyham, on 25 March 1950.

Above: On 1 April 1950 Maunsell Q class No.30540 is photographed again. This time with an interesting train forming the 9.06 am from Three Bridges to Tunbridge Wells West which has just departed from Withyham.

Above: Approaching Withyham on 1 April 1950 is ex-SECR class L No.31779 with the 10.06 am departure from Tunbridge Wells West to Victoria, composed of a rake of Maunsell corridor stock. The class L's were introduced for express passenger working in 1914, and were designed with input from Wainwright, Robert Surtees and Maunsell. No.31779 was one of ten locomotives ordered from A.Borsig & Co. of Berlin and delivered just before the outbreak of World War One.

Above: Geoffrey is closer to Withyham station on 21 April 1951 for this view of class E4 No.32582 entering the station past the headshunt for the goods yard with the 11.30 am train from Tunbridge Wells West to Three Bridges. Note the ex-LBSCR slotted post signal still in use.

Left: No.32582 again this time with the 11.30 am from Tunbridge Wells West to Three Bridges near Withyham on 16 June 1951. Note that the coaches have been repainted in BR 'Blood and Custard' livery.

Right: The Saturdays only 12.47 pm London Bridge to Tunbridge Wells West departs Withyham at 2.18 pm on 4 March 1950 with Q class No.30534 in charge. There was no passing loop at Withyham just a single platform with through and bay roads, along with a small goods yard.

Left: Heading west class I3 No.32021 steams towards Hartfield with the 1.08 pm from Tunbridge Wells West to London Bridge on 16 June 1951. If this was in colour there would probably be an interesting variety of liveries in the mixed coaching stock.

Above: After Hartfield class I3 No.32075 heads towards Forest Row with the 1.08 pm from Tunbridge Wells West to London Bridge on 12 May 1951.

Above: Class E4 No.32582 was clearly a regular on the route as it appears here once more. This time in the woods between Hartfield and Forest Row with the 3.28 pm goods from Tunbridge Wells West to Three Bridges on 28 July 1951.

Left: No.32582 is seen once more climbing Brambletye Bank west of Forest Row with the 3.28 pm freight from Tunbridge Wells West to Three Bridges on 12 May 1951. The bank was a place Geoffrey felt he could get interesting photographs, and so captured several images there.

Right: Later the same day class I3 No.32026 climbs the bank with the 6.12 pm from Tunbridge Wells West to Three Bridges.

Left: It's faster going down with No.32582 (again!) descending the bank with the 2.39 pm Three Bridges to Tunbridge Wells West on 14 July 1951. The passenger stock was set no.230 which consisted of Maunsell brake thirds nos. 2763 and 2764 along with composite no.5673.

Above: The Tunbridge Wells to Three Bridges line used the high level station at East Grinstead. Here class D3 No.2390 propels the 2.34 pm push and pull working from Oxted to Tunbridge Wells West out of East Grinstead on 2 April 1949.

Above: On what was clearly a better day class D No.1730 stands at the western end of East Grinstead High Level station with the 1.08 pm from Tunbridge Wells West to London Bridge on 19 February 1949. Note the shunting signals at the foot of the signal post.

Tunbridge Wells West to Eastbourne

Back to Tunbridge Wells West and another route Geoffrey covered was the one between there and Hailsham. He also made trips to Eastbourne, the destination of many of the trains on this route, where he photographed some of the locos on shed.

On 3 August 1868 the LBSCR opened a line from Groombridge to Uckfield. This connected at Groombridge with the line to Tunbridge Wells from East Grinstead opened on 1 October 1866. Then in the 1870s they promoted a line to run from Redgate Mill Junction via Heathfield to Hailsham.

At Hailsham it would join the line to Polegate and thence to Eastbourne that had been opened on 14 May 1849. The first stage between Hailsham and Heathfield opened on 5 April 1880, with the section from Heathfield to Redgate Mill following on 1 September 1880.

Although the line was built by the LBSCR, the SER claimed a share of the London to Eastbourne traffic. Intermediate stations between Redgate Mill and Hailsham were provided at Rotherfield, Mayfield, Heathfield, Waldron and Hellingly. It became known as the 'Cuckoo Line'.

The line remained single track and was never electrified. But when the route between Redgate Mill and Eridge was doubled in 1894, the Eastbourne line, which ran parallel with the Uckfield track between Redgate Mill and Groombridge, became the down line.

In the 1960s closure was on the cards. The route north of Hailsham was closed to passengers on 14 June 1965, although goods services continued from Heathfield until 26 April 1968. Finally the line between Hailsham and Polegate closed completely on 9 September 1968.

However, the line between Birchden Junction and Tunbridge Wells West remained open until 1985. The section between Redgate Mill and Birchden Junction is still open as part of the route between Oxted and Uckfield, the line from there to Lewes having closed in 1969.

Happily since 1985 the line between Tunbridge Wells and Eridge has been revived as the Spa Valley Railway.

Above: A Brighton-built locomotive, BR standard class 4 2-6-4T No.80018, was one of 130 of the class constructed at the works there. Geoffrey photographed it just south of Birchden Junction on 14 April 1952 with the 1.50 pm from Tunbridge Wells West to Eastbourne. At Birchden Junction the line to Oxted, opened in 1914, continued to the upper left, while diverging to the right was the route to Tunbridge Wells West.

Above: Class H 4-4-0T No.31520 heads north onto the line to Tunbridge Wells at Birchden with the 12.58 pm from Oxted to Tunbridge Wells West on 18 November 1952. This usually worked directly between Ashurst and Groombridge, but according to Geoffrey's notes it was apparently diverted via Eridge on this occasion due to the Point to Point horse races there.

Above: On the same day a more conventional working was the 3.11 pm from Tunbridge Wells West to Lewes pulled by Q class No.30546 seen here between Birchden and Eridge.

Above: Beyond Redgate Mill Junction the line became single track, and here class I3 No.32030 is seen with the 7.52 am from Eastbourne to Tunbridge Wells West on 26 June 1950. The track at this point was on a grade of 1 in 56.

Above: Further south the line passed through woods near Heathfield Hall on the approach to Rotherfield, and here class H No.31182 is seen with the 9.06 am from Tunbridge Wells West to Eastbourne on 22 June 1950.

Left: Beyond Rotherfield there were a series of climbs and descents often on a gradient of about 1 in 50. Mayfield was the next station reached, and then Heathfield. After this came Waldron and Horam, formerly Horeham Road. Here on 28 May 1949 Geoffrey came across class C2 No.2436 shunting the 2.45 pm goods from Tunbridge Wells.

Right: Having shunted its train No.2436 waits in the station to depart. This loco was never to receive BR number or livery as it was withdrawn from service in January 1950. It was also one of only three locomotives of the C2 class taken into BR stock.

Left: Geoffrey had now travelled further down the line going through the station at Hellingly to Hailsham. Here he photographed a familiar train, still in the same formation, which has just passed through the station with the Hailsham South box in the background.

Above: A general view of Hailsham station and goods yard taken the same day with Q class No.546 departing with the 4.35 pm from Tunbridge Wells to Eastbourne. Hailsham South box was one of the first LBSCR standard boxes designed by T.H. Myres, and contained a 22-lever frame. It was commissioned when the line north to Heathfield was opened.

Above: Beyond Hailsham the route ran to Polegate where it joined the main line between Brighton, Eastbourne and Hastings. Trains bound for Eastbourne headed south after Polegate passing through Hampden Park before reaching its destination. This was a place Geoffrey had visited much earlier in his photographic travels, when the station was still under the Southern. Here on 9 August 1947 he photographed Robert Billinton designed class B4 4-4-0 No.2068 built in 1901.

Above: Also in the yard that day was another Robert Billinton locomotive class E5 No.2594, built in 1904 and originally named *Shortbridge* For a brief period between 1938 and 1939 it was fitted with motor gear for push and pull working.

Above: On 23 October 1948 he photographed the Marsh designed *Atlantic* 4-4-2 tank class I1x No.2009. It was originally constructed as a class I1 in 1907 and rebuilt as a class I1x in December 1929.

East Grinstead to Lewes

Most of the route between East Grinstead and Lewes is now part of the Bluebell Railway, the world's first standard gauge preserved railway to operate a public service. However, when Geoffrey was taking his photographs of the line, it was still very much part of the BR network, with seemingly no prospect of the route being closed.

The line itself was built as the Lewes and East Grinstead Railway. It was opened on 1 August 1882, running from Culver Junction on the Lewes to Uckfield line to a new station at East Grinstead, East Grinstead (Low Level). In 1884 a new route was opened by the LBSCR running from East Grinstead to East Croydon via Oxted (already mentioned), and this formed an end-on connection with the Lewes and East Grinstead.

Between East Grinstead and Horsted Keynes, and then along the route to Haywards Heath via Ardingly the route was built as double track. However, south of Horsted Keynes to Culver Junction it was single. Stations were provided at Kingscote, West Hoathly, Horsted Keynes, Sheffield Park, Newick & Chailey, and Barcombe.

The line from Haywards Heath to Horsted Keynes via Ardingly was electrified in 1935, but the remainder of the line remained the preserve of steam. With the coming of nationalisation initially little changed on the route, but in the early 1950s that the first rumblings about the future of the line were heard.

It would be on 28 May 1955 that the line was first closed, but a legal loophole led to its reopening on 7 August 1956. However, it finally succumbed on 17 March 1958.

This was not to be the end of the story, because a preservation society had been formed. It established a base at Sheffield Park station and built up a collection of locomotives and rolling stock. Eventually in the summer of 1960 it operated its first passenger trains from there. Since then it has reopened the line in stages from Sheffield Park, recreating the atmosphere of the days of steam. In fact the line regularly features in television programmes and films. Finally in 2013 it was able to reopen the line all the way from Sheffield Park to East Grinstead, making it possible to travel much of the line just as Geoffrey did in the 1950s.

Above: Sadly little of this scene remains as class C2x No.2534 prepares to leave for Lewes with the 3 pm departure on 19 February 1949. Also in the photo are two sets of ex-SECR 'Birdcage' stock, so named because of the look-outs provided for the guards over the roofs of the carriages, which can be seen in the photo.

Above: On the double track section of the line just south of West Hoathly Geoffrey photographed class U1 No.31894 heading to Brighton with the 12.03 pm train from Victoria on 15 October 1949. The train will just have passed through the 731 yard long Sharpthorne tunnel.

Above: On the same day he had moved slightly further down the line just north of Horsted Keynes and here class E4 No.32516 is seen heading the 3 pm train from East Grinstead to Lewes. It is interesting to compare the differences in the headcodes between the two trains.

Above: Further south again on the single track section just north of Newick & Chailey station class C2x No.32437, originally built in 1893, hauls the 8.32 am goods from Lewes to Kingscote on 18 February 1950.

Above: Later at the same spot class H2 No 32421 *South Foreland* heads to Brighton with the 8.03 am from London Bridge. It is worth noting that both locomotive and carriages are in BR livery, although No.32421 does not have a BR totem on its tender. The locomotive also sports another headcode variation for this line.

Above and Below: During the course of one day on a line Geoffrey would see the same locomotive on different duties, as is the case in these two pictures. In the top photo class C2x No.32437 is seen with the 1.20 pm goods from Kingscote to Lewes near Barcombe on 30 June 1950. Later the same day it is seen returning from Lewes with the 4.03 pm passenger working for Horsted Keynes.

Above: Further south again the line curved south west to join the Lewes to Uckfield line at Culver Junction. Here class E4 No.32494 is seen with the 1.20 pm goods from Kingscote on 30 July 1949.

Above: A little later another class E4 No.32516 passes with the 3 pm from East Grinstead to Lewes.

Above: Class C2 No.2533, one of the other unconverted class C2s, is still in Southern livery on 12 November 1949 as it approaches Culver Junction with the 1.20 pm goods from Kingscote to Lewes. This could certainly be described as a mixed goods train.

Above: Class U1 No.31894 rounds the curve to Culver Junction with the 12.03 pm from Victoria to Brighton on 27 June 1950. Interestingly the final carriage appears to be a Pullman brake, possibly on its way to Preston Park for maintenance.

Above: Another member of the three-cylinder U1 class No.31892 heads north from Culver Junction past the down home on 30 June 1950 with the 5.18 pm Brighton to Victoria working.

Above: Class E4 No.32508 also heads north from the junction with the 6.58 pm from Lewes to Newick & Chailey on 2 June 1951.

Left: At Culver Junction the line joined the Lewes to Uckfield line for the run down to Lewes. This gave Geoffrey the chance to photograph trains on two lines. Therefore, class D3 No.2384, still in Southern livery, is captured with a full head of steam on the 3.11 pm from Tunbridge Wells West to Lewes on 30 July 1949.

Right: Class I3 No.32082 is seen passing Culver Junction, which was named after the nearby farm, with the 12.02 pm from Tunbridge Wells West to Brighton on 12 November 1949.

Left: Later on the same day the sun came out as class D No.31591 passes the junction with the 12.36 pm from Tunbridge Wells West.

Above: Now near Lewes class C2x No.32434 is seen with the 7.28 pm from Newick & Chailey to Lewes on 21 July 1951.

Above: At the same spot BR standard class 4 tank No.42103, on the 7.34 pm train from Brighton to Tunbridge Wells West, is seen with class H2 No. 32426 *St Alban's Head* with the 7.07 pm East Grinstead to Lewes on 21 July 1951.

Keymer Junction to Lewes

The route between Keymer Junction and Lewes was a busy one, being double tracked throughout. Although it had been electrified for many years Geoffrey made several visits to it and had a favourite spot just to the south-east of Cooksbridge station. Here he could photograph the steam worked boat trains from Newhaven in particular.

Completed on 1 October 1847 the line enabled trains from London direct access to Lewes and Newhaven instead of having to travel via Brighton. It departs from the London to Brighton line at Keymer Junction where there was a station until 1883. This was replaced by a second station just to the north in 1886, which was later renamed Wivelsfield. There are two intermediate stations at Plumpton, opened in June 1863, and Cooksbridge, originally Cook's Bridge, opened with the line in 1847.

Electrification took place in 1935, with the electric service operating from the July. This included the lines through to Eastbourne, Hastings and Seaford, which also served Newhaven Harbour and the steamer services to France. However, there were still significant numbers of steam workings, including the Newhaven boat trains, and also through trains from the Midlands and north of England.

Above: Although this book is primarily about Southern steam in the post-war period, part of the change that was going on at that time was in motive power that was being employed. Hence we have Geoffrey's picture of Co-Co Electric 20002, formerly CC2, near Ditchling Common with the 4.14 pm boat train from Newhaven Harbour to Victoria on 19 April 1952.

This locomotive was one of a class of three, two built by the Southern and one by BR, designed by Oliver Bulleid and Alfred Raworth. The first of the class, CC1, was built in 1941, with CC2 not completed until 1945. They were similar in design, but with modifications. No.20003 was built in 1948 and had a different look, as will be seen later.

All three locomotives were designed to use third-rail pick-ups, using flywheels to overcome the problem of momentary power loss. They were also fitted with pantographs to pick up current from overhead lines in sidings. No.20002 lasted in service until December 1968.

Above: Earlier the same day Geoffrey had been further down the line at Spatham Lane crossing. Here he photographed *Battle of Britain* class No.34068 *Kenley* heading up towards London Victoria with the 3.48 pm boat train from Newhaven Harbour.

Above: A little way down the line again he captured this photograph of *Atlantic* class H2 No.32425 *Trevose Head* near Plumpton with the 5.48 pm boat train from Newhaven Harbour to Victoria on 16 June 1951.

Left: As mentioned earlier, just south-east of Cooksbridge station was one of Geoffrey's favourite spots. It was here that he captured No.20003, the third of the Bulleid designed Co-Co electrics in charge of a boat train from Newhaven on 16 July 1949. The differences in the design of the body between the later BR-constructed 20003 and the SR-built 20002 are very much apparent.

Right: More traditional motive power was in charge of the 6.14 pm boat train that day in the form of class U1 *Mogul* No.31909. The loco crew seems keen to get in the photo.

Left: Another day, another boat train, but the same location. This time its *Atlantic* class H2 No.32426 *St Alban's Head*, still in full Southern livery, in charge of the 6.14 pm from Newhaven on 30 July 1949.

Left: Geoffrey took this view slightly closer to Cooksbridge station. It shows the catch points on the siding as class N No.31412, one of the last batch of the class built, passes with the 5.58 pm boat train for Victoria on 20 August 1950.

Right: Another class H2 *Atlantic*, No.32422 *North Foreland*, passes the same spot with the 6.27 pm special on 21 July 1951.

Left: Moving nearer to Lewes this view of *Atlantic* class H2 No.32426 *St Alban's Head*, now repainted in BR livery, was taken just west of Hamsey Crossing on 7 July 1951 with the 6.48 pm from Newhaven. The crossing signal box can be seen in the background. This was opened in 1900, and remained in use until July 1964.

Lewes to Newhaven

The line from Lewes to Newhaven actually extended through to Seaford. However, as the stretch between Newhaven and Seaford was an exclusively electric passenger operation at the time Geoffrey was photographing, he seems only to have ventured as far as Newhaven.

In truth this route was a branch from just east of Southerham bridge on the Lewes and Hastings line. Initially it was only built through to the wharf at Newhaven harbour, opening on 6 December 1847 with double track throughout, but on 1 June 1864 it was extended to Seaford.

Originally it only had stations at Newhaven Town and Wharf. However, in 1906 a halt was opened at Southease and Rodmell. Between Newhaven and Seaford there was one intermediate station at Bishopstone. Although it was a short line it carried significant traffic, not least in connection with the Newhaven and Dieppe ferries.

Later improvements at Newhaven included rebuilding the old wharf station, the new station being known as Newhaven Harbour (or Newhaven Harbour Hotel). In addition, a new continental station for accessing the boats was constructed at the end of a short branch from the Harbour station. The new facilities being opened on

17 May 1886.

In 1904 the line between Newhaven and Seaford was doubled, with the work being completed on 24 July that year. The First World War obviously had a significant impact, and some 19,750 special goods trains were worked to Newhaven during the conflict.

To cope with this increase in traffic ten new goods reception roads were laid on the down side of the line north of Newhaven Town station. These were controlled by a new signal box, Newhaven Town North (renamed Newhaven Town 'A' in 1940).

Grouping brought some changes to the branch. In 1926 the SR took over the property of the Newhaven Harbour Commissioners including a tramroad down to the west breakwater. The route between Southerham and Seaford was also electrified in 1935.

Following nationalisation the line to the continental platform was electrified in 1947, with the last regular steam-hauled boat train running on 14 May 1949. In 1973 the line between Newhaven Harbour and Seaford was singled, and later still the continental station was renamed Newhaven Marine in 1984. However, the latter has been effectively closed since 2006.

Above: Over time Lewes became a major railway centre with lines converging on the town from Brighton, Haywards Heath, East Grinstead, Oxted and Hastings. Not surprisingly the main station had to adapt to the changes. The station above was the third to serve the town. Here Geoffrey photographs class H No.31517 shunting at the Brighton end of the station on 21 July 1951 near to Lewes South signal box.

Southerham Bridge just outside Lewes provided a vantage point to watch some of the inter-regional services cross the River Ouse. Geoffrey took advantage of this and so we have a selection of the photos he took.

Left: Here class U *Mogul* No.31802 crosses the bridge with the 11.40 am from Birmingham New Street to Hastings on 19 August 1950. Off of this photo to the right lies Southerham Junction where the branch for Newhaven and Seaford leaves the Hastings line. In the background is Lewes itself.

Right: On the same day class L1 No.31787 crosses the bridge with the 12.30 pm departure from Leicester (London Road) to Hastings. In the right background was a chalk pit which was active until 1981. For many years it was served by a private tramway which left the main line by a trailing connection also just off to the right of this photo.

Left: Class K *Mogul* No.32347 crosses the viaduct on 7 July 1951 with the 10.40 am Saturdays only from Birmingham Snow Hill to Hastings. The bridge was rebuilt in the 1930s following a collision with a barge.

Right: As mentioned opposite, a private track existed into the Eastwoods Cement Co. works for many years. Here Hawthorn Leslie works no.2532 of 1902 *Atlas No.17*, which came to the works at Lewes around 1932 from the firm of Firth Brown Ltd of Sheffield, is seen bringing a couple of vans into the exchange sidings at Southerham on 19 April 1952.

Left: Class C2x No.32523 passes Newhaven 'A' box with a freight bound for Newhaven Town on 1 July 1950. The signal box was opened in 1917 as part of the improvements to cope with increased traffic during the First World War.

Right: *Atlantic* class H2 No.2425 *Trevose Head* passing Newhaven Town with the 6.14 pm train from Newhaven Harbour to Victoria on 11 June 1949.

Left: Geoffrey was present for the last regular steam-hauled boat train from the continental station at Newhaven Harbour at 5.55 pm on 14 May 1949. Here he photographed the loco crew.
Left to right are Driver Dick Barber, Loco Inspector Jack McCarthy and Fireman Stan Thomas. All standing beside *Schools* class V No.30929 *Malvern*.

Right: For many years at Newhaven there were two tramways which served wharves on the west side of the River Ouse. One was owned by the Earl of Sheffield and linked Meeching quarry with the waterside. The other had been built by the Newhaven Harbour Company in 1893.
This left the main line just north of Newhaven Town station and crossed the Ouse on a swingbridge. It then followed the line of the west bank of the river down to the lighthouse, a distance of one and three-quarter miles. The line became part of the Southern Railway in 1926 when the SR purchased the Harbour Company, and it survived until 1963.
On 23 October 1948 *Terrier* No.2636, then still in Southern livery, heads up to the junction with the main line having crossed the swing bridge. Geoffrey captures it passing the Railway Hotel.

Left: *Terrier* No.2636 had originally been built by the LBSCR in 1872 as No.72 *Fenchurch*. In 1898 it was sold to the Newhaven Harbour Co. for use on the branch. When the Southern took over in 1926 it became No.636 (later No.2636) and lasted in service with the SR and BR until 1964. It was then sold to the Bluebell Railway for preservation where it remains.

Brighton Shed

Above: Many of Geoffrey's early photographs were taken on shed visits, and he made several to the one at Brighton, which have been included in chronological order, illustrating the changes taking place over the years. Class K 2-6-0 No.2339 is seen here on 29 June 1946. It entered service in March 1914, one of a class of goods locomotives designed for the LBSCR by L.B. Billinton, of which 17 were eventually built. No.2339 was modified to fit the Southern's composite gauge in 1936 and is seen here in black with 'Sunshine' lettering. At this time it was still fitted with a Weir pump injection system.

Right: On 28 June 1947 class D1/M 0-4-2 tank No.2252 stands at Brighton with class C2x No.2528 seen behind. Originally built by Neilson & Co for the LBSCR. No.2252 entered service in January 1882 named *Buckhurst*. During World War Two it had been converted for fire-fighting, but by this time had been returned to normal duties.

Left: The class H1 *Atlantics* were one of Douglas Marsh's most iconic locomotives. No.2038 was built by Kitsons in 1905, part of the original batch of five, and named *Portland Bill* by the Southern in 1925. It was adapted for the Southern's composite gauge in 1935 and fitted with a superheater in 1938. By the time of this photo on 24 July 1948 it had been repainted in malachite green, a livery it retained until it was withdrawn in 1951.

Right: The class D3 0-4-4 tanks were introduced by Robert Billinton for the outer suburban passenger services with No. 32398 originally entering traffic in 1896 named *Haslemere*. Although renumbered by British Railways it was not to survive long in their service being withdrawn in March 1949 only a few months after this photo on 24 July 1948.

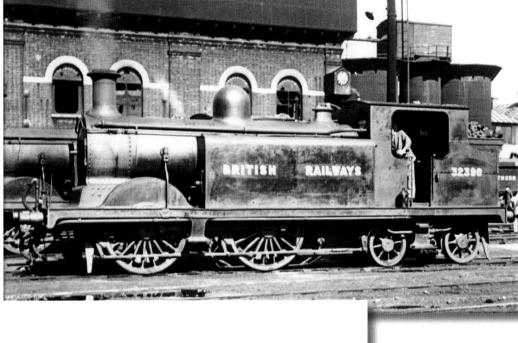

Left: On the same day Geoffrey photographs class E6 No.32415 having just been repainted in British Railways unlined black. Designed by Robert Billinton for suburban goods services where there was the requirement for rapid acceleration, most of the class E6s remained around London for much of their working life. No.32415 was built in 1905 and withdrawn in 1961.

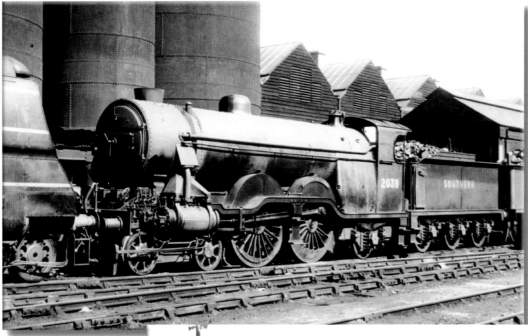

Left: Another H1 class *Atlantic*, this time No.2039 *Hartland Point*, photographed again on 24 July 1948. No.2039, which the LBSCR had used in earlier days as its royal locomotive, had been fitted in November 1947 with a new experimental sleeve-valve gear, multiple-jet blastpipe and chimney. This was to allow it to act as a test-bed for some of the proposed developments for Bulleid's *Leader* class locomotives.

Nationalisation in 1948 meant that for some time locomotives could be seen in a number of different liveries. This is illustrated here by these two photographs taken by Geoffrey on 24 July 1948 of two class C2x locos. No.2528 (right) is still in its Southern livery, while No.2546 (below) had already been repainted into unlined BR black and received the '3'

prefix to its number. The class C2x's had been converted by Marsh from Robert Billinton's class C2 goods locomotives by the substitution of a larger boiler. No.2528 had originally been built in 1900 and converted in 1911, while No.32546 was first built in 1902 and converted in 1912, at this time they both carried singled domed boilers.

Above: Another livery variation with class B4x No.2060 having received an 'S' prefix to its number as part of the early BR changes. The 4-4-0 B4x's were a superheated version of Robert Billinton's class B4 passenger locomotives. No.2060 was originally constructed in 1901 and superheated in 1922. It is seen here on 24 July 1948.

Above: A post-Grouping Brighton-built locomotive. *West Country* class No.34006 *Bude* built in 1945 was photographed by Geoffrey on 14 August 1948.

Above: From a main line express engine to one of the smallest locomotives on the Southern the ex-SECR 'P' class represented by No.1325. It was built in 1910 and was still in its Maunsell livery in this photograph taken by Geoffrey on 14 August 1948. In 1946 it had been loaned to the Kent and East Sussex Railway and lasted in service until 1960.

Above: Class E5 0-6-2 tank No.2587, aptly named *Brighton* when it was built as a secondary passenger and suburban locomotive to a design by Robert Billinton in 1903, is seen on 9 October 1948. It was briefly modified by Marsh to a 2-4-2T by the removal of the front section of the coupling rods, but was soon restored to an 0-6-2T.

Above and Below: Marsh designed his 4-6-2 class J1 locomotives in 1910 for express passenger services. Originally authorisation was given for six to be built, but due to Marsh's illness and retirement only two were constructed. The first was No.325 originally named *Abergavenny* and was fitted with Stephenson valve gear. It is seen here at 3.25 pm, according to the clock (below), on 26 February 1949 when it had recently been repaired and repainted at Brighton works. This followed an accident at Lewes on 13 November 1948 when it had been completely derailed and mounted a platform ramp. Although repainted in green and renumbered No.32325 it never carried any lettering for British Railways until it was withdrawn from service in 1951. The number on the rear of the bunker appeared on some locos in the early days of British Railways.

Tunbridge Wells West Shed

Above: Another of Geoffrey's early photographic expeditions was to the shed at Tunbridge Wells West still under the jurisdiction of the Southern on 29 June 1946. Here he photographed class I3 No.2029 in the foreground and class E4 No.2582 in the shed. An interesting discussion seems to be taking place on the left.

Right: Class J2 No.2326 was completed in 1912 by L.B. Billinton who had included a number of modifications, most obvious of which was the use of Walschaerts valve gear as opposed to the Stephenson gear on No.325 (see opposite). When first in service No.2326 was named *Bessborough*. It is also seen here on 29 June 1946.

Left: Class D3 0-4-4 tank No.2393, designed by Robert Billinton, is prepared for the day's duties on 9 August 1947, with a bunker heaped full of coal. No.2393 dated from 1896 and would last in service until 1951.

Right: A line-up of ex-LBSCR tanks at Tunbridge Wells West shed on 9 August 1947. Nearest the camera is Robert Billinton designed class E5 0-6-2T No.2406 built in 1904. Next to it is class I1x No.2001 a Marsh designed 4-4-2T built in 1907, while furthest from the camera is class I3 4-4-2T No.2028 built in 1909. Marsh disapproved of using locomotives with front-coupled wheels for any passenger duties hence his range of *Atlantic*-type tanks.

Left: The most successful of the Marsh *Atlantic* tanks was undoubtedly the I3 class and No.2076 was built in 1910. Originally it was not superheated until the Southern fitted a new boiler in 1927. It is seen here on 17 May 1948.

Newhaven Shed

Right: Geoffrey also visited the shed at Newhaven several times, the first of which was on 3 May 1947. Then class H2 No.2426 *St Alban's Head* is seen in malachite green livery outside the shed. This shot well illustrates the severe 90 degree curve on the access from the main line.

Above: Ex-LBSCR class C2 No.2533, another of the three class C2 locomotives to enter BR stock, stands in the shed yard on 6 June 1949. In February 1950 it was withdrawn having run over a million miles.

Left: Illustrating the livery changes that were taking place over this period on 14 May 1949 are *Terrier* No.2636, previously seen on p.52, still in Southern livery, and class E4 No.32494 in early BR lined black, but without a totem on the tanks.

Right: On 18 February 1950 K class *Mogul* No.32346 stands on the turntable in front of the shed complete with the early version of the BR Totem applied to its tender, which was used up until 1956.

Left: Having been turned No. 32346 stands ready for duty again with the gasworks behind it.

Right: Before heading down to the Harbour station to haul the last regular steam hauled boat train Geoffrey captures No.30929 *Malvern* standing in the loco yard on 14 May 1949.

Left: Newhaven loco shed backed on to the River Ouse at ninety degrees to the main line. Here on 1 July 1950 class H2 No.2425 *Trevose Head* can be seen still in its old Southern livery. Meanwhile *Terrier* No.32636, seen opposite in Southern livery, has now been repainted in fully lined BR livery, and is having its smoke box cleaned.

Right: Inside Newhaven shed on 16 July 1949 with *Terrier* No.2647, formerly LBSCR No.47 *Cheapside*. It was only to last in service another three years being withdrawn in October 1952 due to a broken crank axle.

Whitstable Harbour

Geoffrey's visit to the harbour at Whitstable took place on 13 May 1950, and gives a flavour of the area in its final years. It was also the start of an interesting day out which took him from the north Kent coast to the south Kent coast. Along the way he also visited the Hythe branch capturing the scene on the rear cover, before finishing the day on the New Romney branch, as will be seen in the next section.

The Canterbury and Whitstable Railway was famed because when it opened, in 1830, it was the first steam-worked passenger line in the south-east of England. It linked the city of Canterbury to the harbour on the Thames estuary at Whitstable. This included the line passing through the world's first railway tunnel used by passenger trains at Tyler Hill.

In fact the line was only partially steam-worked with originally two, later three, cable worked inclines along its length, with the first locomotive *Invicta* only working at the Whitstable end of the line. Gravity working was also employed including for passenger trains.

However, in 1844 the South Eastern Railway took over the line, and instituted a major series of improvements. This included the use of steam locomotives along the length of the line, as well as linking the line to the wider railway network.

The restricted loading gauge of the tunnel at Tyler Hill limited the locomotives that could be used on the line. Therefore eventually class R (later R1) locomotives, that had been especially cut-down for use on the line, were employed.

These continued in service after the Southern took over in 1923. In 1931 the passenger service was discontinued and finally the line closed on 1 December 1952, although it did reopen briefly due to flooding in 1953. Its closure caused sufficient a stir that it was even mentioned in the Ealing comedy film *The Titfield Thunderbolt*, which was based on the preservation of the Talyllyn Railway.

Above: The use of modified class R, later R1, locomotives on the line has been mentioned above. Three of the R class, Nos. 10, 77 and 147, were built with short chimneys for use on the line in 1890 and No.124 was also fitted out for use on the line in 1893. Over the years there were changes to the numbers of the class allocated to the line. Many of the class were also modified with H class boilers to become class R1s. By August 1945 Nos. 1010, 1069, 1147 and 1339 were altered for use on the line, Nos.1069 and 1339 being fitted with rounded Stirling pattern cabs. No.1339 is seen here during Geoffrey's visit in 1950 still in Southern livery.

Above: No.1339 is seen shunting at Whitstable harbour near the site of the original 1830 passenger station.

Above: No.1339 shunting beside the former Whitstable Harbour passenger station, which had replaced the original 1830 station in 1894, but was closed in 1931.

The New Romney Branch

The New Romney branch had an interesting history. Originally the line was opened between Appledore and Lydd, with an intermediate station at Brookland, by the Lydd Railway Company (LRC) on 7 December 1881. There was also a line to Dungeness opened for goods on the same day, and for passengers from 1 April 1883. This was hoped to be the first stage in developing a major port at Dungeness, but this proved to be an abortive plan.

In 1882 the company was authorised to build a line from Lydd to New Romney and also from Appledore to Headcorn via Tenterden. A further Act of 1883 authorised an extension from Headcorn to Loose near Maidstone. Eventually only the New Romney line was built, opening on 19 June 1884, while the LRC became part of the SER in 1895.

South of Lydd there was a military camp and firing range served by a connection from the branch opened in 1883. This lasted until the 1920s. Like other branches in the area, Kitson steam railmotors were introduced in 1906 to save money. During the First World War the area was obviously strategically significant, with large numbers of troop movements to and from Lydd camp.

Following the Grouping the SR also sought to save money by employing a four-wheeled petrol-engined Drewry railcar, as well as a French *Micheline* which ran on rubber-tyred flanged wheels in 1930. It also reduced Brookland station to the status of a halt, and withdrew the passenger service to Dungeness in 1937.

By this time another addition to the area was the miniature Romney, Hythe and Dymchurch Railway, opened between Hythe and New Romney in 1927 and extended to Dungeness the following year. At the same time there was a series of major developments in the

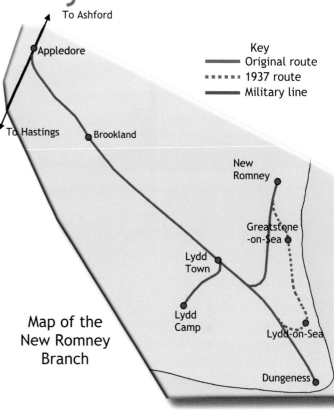

Map of the New Romney Branch

Key
— Original route
···· 1937 route
— Military line

area, including the establishment of two holiday camps. As a result the SR re-aligned the route between Lydd and New Romney nearer to the coast. This included opening two halts at Lydd-on-Sea and Greatstone-on-Sea, with the new section of track coming into use on 4 July 1937.

The branch was on the front line during the Second World War. In 1943 a train was attacked by a German aircraft. Following nationalisation the goods traffic on the Dungeness branch was ended in May 1953. However, subsequently construction of the Dungeness nuclear power station led to the line being retained, and the section between Appledore and Dungeness is still in use today for nuclear traffic.

Meanwhile, steam was replaced by diesel-electric multiple units (DEMUs) in 1962. Goods services to New Romney were withdrawn in 1964. Passenger services were finally withdrawn on 6 March 1967, and goods services to Lydd Town only lasted until 1971.

Left: Geoffrey's day on 13 May 1950 started at Whitstable harbour on the north Kent coast, and ended on the south coast at New Romney. Here he photographed ex-SECR class R1 No.31710 between turns.

Above: Earlier the same day class D3 No.32368 arrives at New Romney with the 4.44 pm from Ashford.

Above: The reason for Geoffrey's visit was an excursion, organised by Ian Allan Ltd, which included a trip along the branch. Therefore to provide extra accommodation a three-coach 'Birdcage' set was being added to the regular branch train by No.32368.

Above: At 5.50 pm the strengthened train departed for Ashford conveying the excursionists.

Above: However, Geoffrey remained at New Romney and recorded the arrival of class R1 No.31710 with the 6.48 pm from Appledore. This then formed the 7.33 pm departure, upon which Geoffrey presumably started his journey home.

Brighton Kemp Town Branch

Above: The LBSCR opened the branch to Kemp Town in Brighton on 2 August 1869. It consisted of just over a mile of track, but had cost over £100,000 and its main purpose had been to prevent the London, Chatham and Dover Railway from gaining access to Brighton. Passenger traffic gradually dwindled, and even a brief experiment with petrol railcars early in the 20th century did not stop passenger services from being withdrawn on 1 January 1933. The line did though remain open for goods until 1971. However, on 5 October 1952 a steam special organised by the Railway Correspondence and Travel Society traversed the branch, and Geoffrey was there to record the scene at the former Kemp Town station.

Above: The train was hauled by *Terrier* No.32636, formerly LBSCR No.72 *Fenchurch*, previously seen at work on the Newhaven harbour branch, and also on shed at Newhaven.

Above: Building the branch involved the construction of two substantial viaducts, and also the digging of the 1024 yd Kemp Town tunnel, the southern portal of which can be seen here as the special prepares to depart. Some of the passengers are clearly anxious not to be left behind. The tunnel portal can still be found at the rear of the industrial estate that now occupies the station site.

Above: The special regains the main line at Kemp Town Junction. It would not be the last passenger train to Kemp Town as at least one more steam special operated on the branch. In addition, the last day the line was in use, on 26 June 1971, a DEMU operated a shuttle service along it.

The Westerham Branch

Strictly speaking the photographs in this section lie outside the time-frame of this book. However, although Geoffrey discovered the Westerham branch later in his photographic career, he was obviously keen to record it making two trips within the space of a few weeks in 1960.

The branch itself became a near survivor of the steam age, although now some of its route lies beneath the tarmac and concrete of the M25. Originally the SER had promised to build a line to Westerham, but when this failed to materialise a local initiative was begun to get the line built.

Known as the Westerham Valley Railway (WVR) it opened on 6 July 1881 from Dunton Green on the SER line to Sevenoaks to Westerham. Almost immediately the WVR was taken over by the SER, who, with their successor the SECR, continued to operate the line until the Grouping.

Some 4½ miles long there was originally only one intermediate station on the branch, at Brasted, although a halt at Chevening was opened later in 1906. The latter event was as a result of the introduction of Kitson railcars on the route, but, as elsewhere, this was fairly short-lived. After Grouping the SR tried a Sentinel steam railcar on the line, but this too did not last long.

During the following years the line continued to operate a service of largely local, often push and pull, trains along the branch.

However, there were also through services operated to London. The winter timetable for the line in 1936 had some 22 departures from Westerham Monday to Friday starting at 6.16 am with the last train from Dunton Green at 11.28 pm. This became the 12.08 am departure on a Saturday (actually of course Sunday morning).

The line survived the war, it even was rumoured that Winston Churchill made use of the branch on journeys to and from Chartwell. However, in 1961 its closure was announced, the last trains running on 28 October 1961.

However, even that was nearly not the end, because a preservation society was established, and very nearly succeeded in re-opening it. However, in the end the projected route of the M25 was to prove its demise.

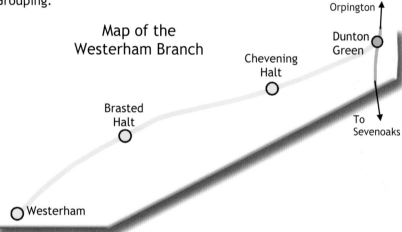

Map of the
Westerham Branch

To Orpington

Dunton Green

Chevening Halt

Brasted Halt

To Sevenoaks

Westerham

Above: Geoffrey captures a classic view of class H No.31500 at Westerham on 15 May 1960 with push and pull set No.723. The advertisements on the left reflect the time period.

Left: No.31500 propels the 3.23 pm train out of Westerham to Dunton Green. The signal box was supplied by Stevens and Co..

Right: Later the same evening Geoffrey photographs No.31500 between Westerham and Brasted with the 5.50 pm from Dunton Green. The class H 0-4-4 tank locomotives were designed by H.S. Wainwright for suburban and semi-fast passenger services, with 66 being built between 1904 and 1915. No.31500 was built in 1905. It had only been fitted for push and pull working a few months before this photo was taken, and only lasted in service until June 1961.

Left: Brasted Halt was supplied with a similar station building to the one at Westerham and a brick built platform. It is seen here looking towards Westerham.

Right: Geoffrey visited the line again on 4 June 1960 and got this photograph of class H No. 31177 in the woods between Brasted and Chevening with the 3.50 pm from Dunton Green. Photos like this show what a picturesque line it was and why it was nearly preserved. Loco No.31177 was built in 1909, and between 1943 and 1944 it had been loaned to the LMS for service in Scotland. It was withdrawn in October 1961, probably following the closure of the branch.

Left: Chevening Halt had been rebuilt in the 1930s utilising the products of the Southern's concrete works at Exmouth. On 4 June 1960 No.31177 is propelling the 4.23 pm from Westerham past the halt.

Right: Changing locomotives at Dunton Green as class H No.31518, standing in the platform, is about to be exchanged for No.31177 on the left. The latter would then depart for Westerham with the 1.05 pm train. This again consisted of push and pull set No.723 made up of ex-LBSCR driving brake third No.3855 and composite No.6250.

The Kent and East Sussex Railway

Geoffrey visited the Kent and East Sussex Railway (K&ESR) on a number of occasions during its final years under British Railways, his first recorded visit taking place in September 1949 and his last in October 1954. These photos therefore provide a fascinating snapshot of the line during this period.

The K&ESR is perhaps the best known of the railways with which the eponymous Col H.F. Stephens was associated. Originally the line opened in 1900 between Robertsbridge, on the SECR's line from Tonbridge to Hastings, and Tenterden (later known as Rolvenden) station. At this time it was known as the Rother Valley Railway.

In March 1903 the line was extended to Tenterden Town. Work had also begun on the line from there to Headcorn on the SECR's line between Tonbridge and Ashford. The following year the railway was renamed the Kent and East Sussex Light Railway, and on 15 May 1905 the extension to Headcorn (or Headcorn Junction as the K&ESR called it) opened.

The railway remained independent through Grouping and even survived the death of Col. Stephens in 1931. By then though the finances of the line were poor, and even the introduction of petrol-driven railcars failed to turn the situation around.

However, the railway survived to the outbreak of the Second World War, mainly due to the cooperation of the Southern Railway, which also hired locomotives to the K&ESR. During the war it came under government control and had a strategically significant role, which meant that it emerged in 1945 with better infrastructure than in 1939.

Nationalised in 1948 its future became uncertain. Regular passenger services ceased on 2 January 1954 when the line between Tenterden and Headcorn also closed. Goods trains continued to run on the remaining section until 12 June 1961 when the line was closed completely save for a short section to Robertsbridge Mill.

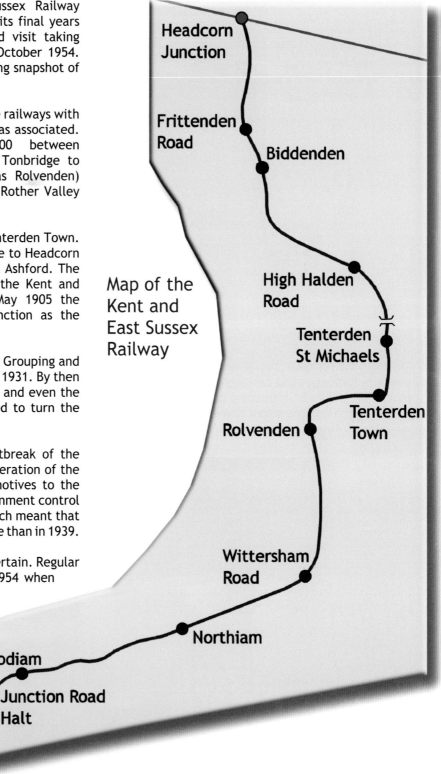

Map of the Kent and East Sussex Railway

However, that was not the end of the story as a band of enthusiasts took up the challenge of preserving the line. The first trains ran between Tenterden and Rolvenden in 1974 and now regular services are run to Bodiam. A separate enterprise, the Rother Valley Railway, is also attempting to rebuild the line between Robertsbridge and Bodiam.

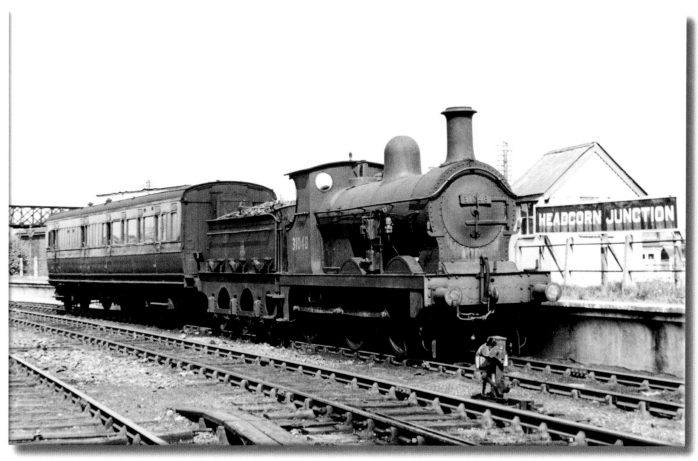

Above: On 26 April 1952 ex-SECR class O1 No.31048 built in 1893 waits at Headcorn Junction with the single coach that will form the 10.55 am to Tenterden Town. The axle loadings of the class O1s were too heavy to allow them to proceed further towards Robertsbridge than Rolvenden, officially.

Above: Freight traffic could still be substantial, as this photo taken on 5 July 1952 of class O1 No.1064 having arrived at Headcorn Junction with the 3.15 pm mixed from Rolvenden shows.

Above: Biddenden was quite a well equipped station complete with a loop, up and down platforms as well as a goods shed. However even these facilities proved inadequate for the annual Biddenden fair when the down platform had to be used as a cattle dock. Class O1 No.31065 is seen at the station with the 12.30 pm from Headcorn Junction to Rolvenden on 11 April 1953.

Above: Beyond Biddenden was High Halden Road, which was a simple halt with two sidings. On 7 November 1953 No.31065 pulls in with the 12.30 pm from Headcorn Junction to Rolvenden.

Right: Further south class O1 No.31048 is seen with the 12.30 pm from Headcorn Junction to Rolvenden on 26 April 1952.

Left: St Michaels tunnel was really a large overbridge carrying the only road to cross the line not on a crossing. It is here on 17 May 1952 that class O1 No.31048 is seen emerging from the north portal with the 11.32 am from Tenterden Town to Headcorn Junction.

Right: On the Tenterden side of the tunnel the small St Michaels halt opened in 1912. It is near here that No.31048 is seen on the same day as previously with the 10.55 am from Headcorn Junction to Tenterden Town.

Right: Tenterden Town station with class O1 No.1064, which has just arrived with the 4.46 pm from Headcorn Junction on 5 July 1952.

Left: Perhaps the iconic view of Tenterden Town, with *Terrier* No.32678 on the road crossing at the Rolvenden end of the station running round its train, with the famous triple-armed signal on the right.

No.32678 had an interesting history. It was originally built by the LBSCR in 1880 as No.78 *Knowle*, but the Southern shipped it over to the Isle of Wight in 1929. Here it became W4 (later W14) *Bembridge*. Returning to the mainland it was hired to the K&ESR in 1940 and remained there until 1954. Happily the locomotive is now back working on the preserved K&ESR.

Right: On 17 May 1952 *Terrier* No.32659 is seen preparing to take some empty stock from Tenterden Town to Rolvenden, which had previously formed the 8.15 am train from Robertsbridge. In the background the *Nissen* huts that can be seen were part of a government emergency supply store.

Above: The sharp curve at the east end of Tenterden Town station is well illustrated here as class O1 No. 31048 runs round its train on 26 April 1952.

Above: Class O1 No.1064 stands on the Rolvenden side of the road crossing at Tenterden Town while running round its train on 5 July 1952.

Above: Having run down No.1064 then prepares to depart with the 6 pm train for Headcorn Junction.

Above: No.31065 shunts the stock off of the 12.30 pm from Headcorn Junction on 11 April 1953. The class Os were originally designed by James Stirling for the SER with the first of the class being delivered in 1878. In total 122 were built between 1878 and 1899. From 1903 59 engines were fitted with larger H class boilers and became known as the O1s, No.31065 was rebuilt as an O1 in 1908 having been originally constructed in 1896. Happily it was preserved and is now based on the Bluebell Railway.

Above and Below: Beyond Tenterden Town is Rolvenden and here *Terrier* No.2640 is seen shunting on 17 September 1949. No.2640 had originally been built by the LBSCR in 1878 as No.40 *Brighton*, and had been a gold medal winner when displayed at the Paris Exhibition the same year. Later it was purchased by the Isle of Wight Central Railway in 1902 where it was to remain as No.11, later W11 *Newport*, until returning to the mainland in 1947. When withdrawn in 1963 it was sold to Butlins for display at their Pwllheli holiday camp until it returned to the Isle of Wight in 1973, where it has since been restored and is now in service on the steam railway.

Above: No.2640 is being coaled on shed at Rolvenden on 17 September 1949. Rolvenden was the original terminus of the Rother Valley Railway before it was extended to Tenterden Town, hence its relatively extensive facilities.

Above: Rolvenden was the limit of working for the class O1s, and here No.31048 arrives with the 8.50 am mixed train from Headcorn Junction via Tenterden on 26 April 1952.

Right: *Terrier* No.32678 departs from Rolvenden for Robertsbridge with the 8.50 am from Headcorn Junction, which it has taken over from No.31048 on 26 April 1952.

Left: On the same day No.31048 is in action again with the 3.15 pm from Rolvenden to Headcorn Junction. A Maidstone and District bus has been made to wait at the crossing.

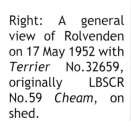

Right: A general view of Rolvenden on 17 May 1952 with *Terrier* No.32659, originally LBSCR No.59 *Cheam*, on shed.

Left: *Terrier* No. 32678, now preserved on the revived K&ESR, shunts at Rolvenden on the evening of 5 July 1952.

Right: No.31065 sports the 'unicycling lion' BR totem on its tender as it shunts the stock for the 3.15 pm mixed train from Rolvenden to Headcorn Junction on 11 April 1953.

Left: Now the train stands in the platform awaiting the departure to Tenterden Town.

Above: Geoffrey photographs *Terrier* No.32678 as it shunts at Wittersham Road in the early afternoon of 28 November 1953. The isolation of the station is clearly seen in this photograph.

Above: On 17 May 1952 *Terrier* No.32659 stands at Northiam station with the 4.15 pm from Tenterden Town to Robertsbridge. The far section of the platform had been raised slightly to allow for the easier loading of milk churns.

Above and Below: A large flour mill at North Bridge near Robertsbridge was served by a siding off of the K&ESR. It is here on 5 July 1952 that No.32678 is seen shunting in this and the following two photos. The flour mill belonged to James Hodson & Sons, Robertsbridge. After the closure of the rest of the K&ESR in 1961 the line to the mill remained open as a private siding. The mill owners purchased ex-SECR class P locomotive No.31556 to work the line, which was renamed *Pride of Sussex*. When rail traffic to the mill ceased on 1 January 1970 the locomotive was sold to the revived K&ESR where it remains.

Above: The road crossing shown above was a something of a safety hazard as it could only be closed to road traffic on one side.

Above: *Terrier* No.32678 has departed from Robertsbridge with the 12.30 pm mixed train for Rolvenden on 5 July 1952.

Above: Geoffrey captures the scene from the footbridge over the main line at Robertsbridge. This shows *Terrier* No.32678 standing in the K&ESR bay platform with the 5.50 pm train for Tenterden Town on 26 April 1952.

Above: Earlier the same day No.32678 stands at Robertsbridge with the 8.15 am train for Tenterden Town. In March 1949 No.32678 was involved in a derailment near Wittersham Road which left it on its side in a marsh, but it was recovered and repaired.

Above and Below: The bay platform at Robertsbridge lacked a loop, and so trains had to be shunted out of the station to allow the locomotive to run round. This is what No.32678 is doing on 5 July 1952 in preparation for the 8.15 am departure to Tenterden Town.

The Kent and East Sussex Railway

Photographers, who developed and printed their own films, will know the frustration when it all went horribly wrong. Evidently when Geoffrey took photos of the last day of passenger operations on 2 January 1954 something went amiss in the developing process. Happily, courtesy of modern digital restoration it has been possible to 'rescue' a few images although the quality is not the best.

Right: Class O1 No.31065 is photographed near Tenterden St Michaels with the 10.55 am from Headcorn to Tenterden Town.

Left: No.31065 again this time leaving St Michaels Tunnel with the 11.32 am from Tenterden Town to Headcorn Junction. This was to be the last day of all operations on this section of the line, while only the section between Tenterden Town station and Robertsbridge remained open for goods.

Right: The rare sight of two trains at Tenterden Town as No.31065 waits with the 12.30 pm from Headcorn Junction to Rolvenden, while *Terrier* No.32655 enters with the 12.30 pm from Robertsbridge, which had been especially extended to Tenterden for the occasion. Some people were seemingly over zealous in seeking a vantage point.

Last Day of the Sheppey Light Railway

The Sheppey Light Railway was another railway that Colonel Stephens was associated with in the area. It was opened on 1 August 1901 running from Queenborough, on the ex-LCDR line between Sittingbourne and Sheerness at the western end of the island, to Leysdown-on-Sea at the eastern end.

From the outset the SECR operated the line, and purchased it in 1904. One innovation they introduced was the use of two Kitson steam railmotors and trailers. These were used on the route between 1905 and 1914. When steam railmotors ceased to be used on the branch their carriage bodies were converted into two articulated carriage sets in the 1920s. These saw service on the branch right up until its closure.

While the railmotors were operating the line the SECR purchased a *Terrier* tank locomotive from the LBSCR, ex-No.54 *Waddon*, which was used for goods services. It became No.751 in the SECR's books and was known locally as 'Little Tich'.

After Grouping the Southern continued to operate the line, and there was even talk of a holiday camp at Leysdown, but this came to nothing. During the Second World War the line's close proximity to Eastchurch Aerodrome led to several bombing incidents on the line. However, the numbers of service personnel using the route ensured that the trains ran throughout the conflict.

But with the return of peace there was a decrease in passenger traffic as the bus and the car provided more attractive forms of transportation, particularly for holidaymakers. After nationalisation an appraisal of the state of the line led to the decision that it should be closed, and the last trains ran on 2 December 1950. It was then that Geoffrey, Ken Carr and others were present to witness the event.

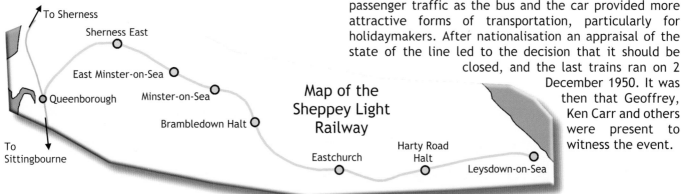

Map of the Sheppey Light Railway

Above: Ex-SECR class R1 0-4-4 No.31705 takes water at Queenborough on 2 December 1950.

Above: No.31705 stands in the bay platform at Queenborough waiting to depart with the 10.55 am departure for Leysdown.

Above: The same train has now arrived at Leysdown, where there is little evidence of the crowds and brass bands that witnessed the last train later in the day. The coaching stock consists of set no.514, one of the two articulated sets rebuilt from the bodies of the steam railmotors.

Left: No.31705 runs round the train at Leysdown. Except for renumbering it is still in its Southern livery at this time. No.31705 was originally built by Sharp, Stewart for the SECR in 1900, but was only to last in service a few more months after this photo was taken. The loco was withdrawn in June 1951.

Right: Having run round the train is now ready to depart as the 11.36 am to Queenborough. Some of the enthusiasts who have come down for the occasion are obviously rushing to make sure they don't miss it.

Left: Geoffrey photographs the train as it arrives at Queenborough for one of the final times.

Last Day of the Hythe Branch

Another branch line, which closed in the early 1950s, that Geoffrey witnessed the last day of, was the Hythe branch. This ran from Sandling, on the former SER line from Ashford to Folkestone, to Hythe and originally on to Sandgate, a distance of 3½ miles. Opened on 9 October 1874 by the Hythe and Sandgate Railway Co. it was unusual for a branch line in that it was laid as double track.

When it was first opened there was no station at Sandling, passenger trains originating from Westenhanger station, but in 1888 Sandling Junction station was opened. This had four platform roads, two for the main line and two for the branch.

However, although there were proposals to extend the line to Folkestone, traffic remained light. When the Southern took over they looked for economies and so in 1931 they closed the line between Hythe and Sandgate and singled the remaining section of line. The branch was even closed for two years during the Second World War.

After nationalisation it was decided to close the branch completely with the final trains running on 1 December 1951. That day Geoffrey turned up to record the event. It was evidently not a good day for photography, nevertheless, these photos represent testimony to the passing of a Southern branch line.

Map of the Hythe Branch

Sandling Junction

To Folkestone

To Ashford and Westenhanger

Hayne Wood Tunnel

Hythe

Sandgate

Above: Ex-SECR class C No.31721 is running round at Hythe, having brought in the 1.50 pm Saturday only working from Ashford. The signal box is a variation on a standard SER design. Of course at this time the line to Sandgate had been closed and the line truncated back to Hythe. The SECR C class locomotives had been designed by H. Wainwright primarily for freight duties, but were also used on passenger turns. It proved a successful design and 109 were eventually built. No.31721 was built by Sharp, Stewart and Co. in 1901, and lasted in service until 1962.

Left: Having run round its train No.31721 prepares to depart with the 2.55 pm Saturdays only to Sandling Junction.

Right: This view shows the slightly run down state of Hythe station. The lack of crowds on this final day of services probably illustrates best why the line was being closed, nevertheless the stationmaster proudly stands on the platform on his last day on duty there.

Left: Clearly the weather had not improved by the time the train had got to Sandling Junction. The locomotive has now run round and is ready to return with the 3.10 pm train to Hythe which again only ran on a Saturday. Normal Monday to Friday services consisted of only three return workings at this time, and no services on a Sunday.

Bibliography

Branch Lines to East Grinstead, V. Mitchell and K. Smith, Middleton Press, 1984

Branches and Byways in Kent, John Scott-Morgan, OPC, 2008

History of the Southern Railway, C.F. Dendy Marshall, Ian Allan Ltd, 1963

Locomotives of the L.B. & S.C.R. Vols 1, 2 & 3, D.L. Bradley, RCTS, 1969, 1972, and 1974

Signal Box Register, Vol.4 Southern Railway, Signalling Record Society, 2009

South Coast Railways: Eastbourne to Hastings, V. Mitchell and K. Smith, Middleton Press, 1986

South Coast Railways: Brighton to Eastbourne, V. Mitchell and K. Smith, Middleton Press, 1985

South Coast Railways: Hastings to Ashford, V. Mitchell and K. Smith, Middleton Press, 1987

Southern Electric 1909-1979, G.T. Moody, Ian Allan Ltd, Fifth Edition 1979

The Kent and East Sussex Railway, S. Garrett, Oakwood Press, 1987

The Locomotive History of the South Eastern and Chatham Railway, D.L. Bradley, RCTS 1980

The Locomotive History of the South Eastern Railway Revised Edition, D.L. Bradley, RCTS, 1985

The London, Brighton and South Coast Railway Vols 1, 2 and 3, J.T. Howard Turner, Batsford, 1977, 1978 and 1979

The Southern in Kent and Sussex, Terry Gough, OPC, 1984

Principle Web Resources

Rail UK at www.railuk.info

Southern E- Group at www.semgonline.com

Subterrania Britannica at www.subbrit.org.uk

Other Books Currently Available From Holne Publishing

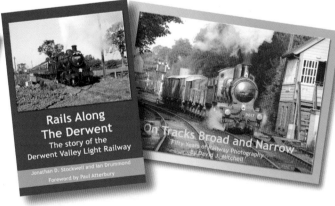

For more information about these or our forthcoming publications visit our website at:
www.holnepublishing.co.uk

or e-mail us at:
enquiries@holnepublishing.co.uk

or write to:
Holne Publishing, PO Box 343,
Leeds, LS19 9FW